Walks
Around Rothbury
and
Coquetdale

By

Kenneth Bunn

TRAIL GUIDES
p u b l i c a t i o n s

First published in Great Britain in 2011 by Trailguides Limited.
www.trailguides.co.uk

ISBN 978-1-905444-48-9

Trailguides Limited
35 Carmel Road South
Darlington
Co Durham DL3 8DQ

Cover design by Steve Gustard.

Dedicated to
All Coquetdale Country Walkers

By the lough. Walk 3 Darden Lough.

CONTENTS

Cover photos.
Front. Dove Crag. Walk 1 The Rothbury Round.
Back. Through Gleadheugh Wood. Walk 4 Rothbury - Fields, Forest and Moor.

INTRODUCTION

1. Rothbury

There are no written words to tell us who lived here in ancient times though the number of hillforts in the area certainly confirm this to have once been a well populated place. Rothbury, the 'Capital of Coquetdale' was first recorded as 'Rodeberia', and in a document dated around 1125, 'Routhebiria', possibly the stronghold of a man named Hrotha. By 1256 it had become 'Roubiry', close to its modern spelling. In 1291 Edward I granted a Charter to hold a market every Thursday, and an annual fair.

The old bridge over the Coquet dates from the 15th century when it was a three arch packhorse bridge, a fourth arch being added in 1759.

The Parish Hall next to the Tourist Information Centre was built in 1908 on the site of the Three Half Moons Public House, where meetings, courts, excise sittings and parish business also took place. In 1715, the Earl of Derwentwater stayed at this public house on his way to defeat during the failed first Jacobite Rebellion. Look for the blue plaque on the wall.

The cross on the village green was erected to the memory of Lord and Lady Armstrong of Cragside in 1902 on the site of an older market cross. Also on the village green, Donkin's unmistakable lamp, gifted by Robert Donkin to commemorate the Coronation of their Gracious Majesties King Edward VII and Queen Alexandra, August 9th, 1902.

All Saints Church was rebuilt in 1850. The Chancel, and part of the transepts are however 13th century.

The old Grammar School for Boys at the corner of Bridge Street and Haw Hill was built in 1841, with an Educational Endowment originally bequeathed in 1720 by the Rev. Tomlinson. It has now been restored as a Cafe and Bunkhouse, appropriately named Tomlinson's.

2. Pubs of Particular Interest

'Walk, and then to think,
Let's eat and drink,
And talk about our walk'

There are three 'pubs' in Rothbury with unique architectural features, so often overlooked unless drawn to your attention.

The Newcastle Hotel, which was once the Black Bull, has an impressive portico entrance.

7

The Queens Head has a relief figure of a queen on the front wall and parts of the building date back to 1790. Formally known as the Golden Fleece it probably became the Queens Head in 1837 to commemorate Queen Victoria's accession to the throne.

Next time you're standing outside The Turks Head, look up to see the 'turks head' figure on the top of the building.

3. The Walks

Coquetdale has some very defined areas of outstanding natural beauty. The walks in this book have been selected to reflect this wide diversity of country-side contrasts, always with something different to see.

To add an extra dimension to your walks, look for birds and wildlife and learn

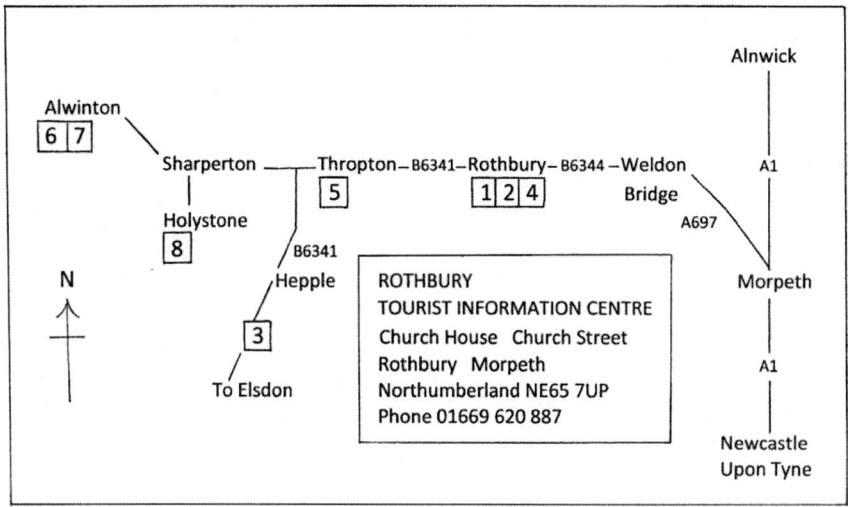

more about historic features. Record your walks so that in the future you'll know exactly where you've been and what you've seen.

This doesn't need to involve long descriptions, just brief notes in a book or on a computer spreadsheet listing dates, titles, and any other relevant information. This will often be enough to recall specific walking days, and with photos you'll build up a personal reference of unforgettable experiences and memories.

I hope you enjoy these walks as much as I have enjoyed putting them together.

4. The Weather

The weather is always a variable factor - just right, too hot, too cold, too wet - sunny in the morning, rain in the afternoon, and the seasons are not always a good indicator. A walk in December with clear blue skies would naturally be preferable to a dull rainy day in June or July. The latest 'ever improving' technical outdoor clothing enables us to adjust to any weather situation, provided of course we assess the conditions on the day, with a good pair of walking boots being obviously essential at all times. Also remember that a waterproof jacket and trousers will be as useful for keeping out the chill factor on a dry day as keeping you dry on a wet day, so always include waterproofs.

5. Safety

You must be prepared for the unexpected. No-one can predict an accident. Whilst you're never likely to forget the sandwiches and flask, at least one person on a walk should carry a basic medi-kit, and mobile phone.

As well as the detailed maps in this book a 25,000 scale OS Map and compass will add interest of any walk, and help keep you on the right path. The more obvious path may not be the right path. A compass calculation could save a lot of unnecessary walking - and keep your route finding reputation intact.

The ability to read a map and calculate a grid reference can also be very useful in an emergency situation.

You can also add to the safety and enjoyment of a walk with walking poles. They power you along on level ground, help push you uphill, take the downhill strain, give you the 'stability of a mountain goat', and greatly reduce the chances of a fall or twisted ankle. You must however, use two poles, one pole is no pole - play it safe.

By Dove Crag. Walk 8 Holystone.

WALK 1: THE ROTHBURY ROUND

This walk is a 'Northumbrian Classic' of many contrasts, so rightly deserves the special title which I have given it. The varied views and scenery are truly spectacular with each section of the route having its own particular interest. There's prehistory and medieval history here, dark forest, a short exhilarating ascent to a 'mountain top' and wild open moorland.

GRADE: F6 [D1, N1, T1,R1,H2]   **DISTANCE:** 7.6 miles (12.2 km)
START: Cowhaugh Car Park   **TIME:** 5 ½ hours app
GRID: NU 057 015   **MAP:** OL42 Kielder Water & Forest

ALONG THE COQUET
From the Car Park, over the footbridge and left with the playground on your right, to pick up a very easy walking well surfaced path all the way to the 'on route' footbridge over the River Coquet.

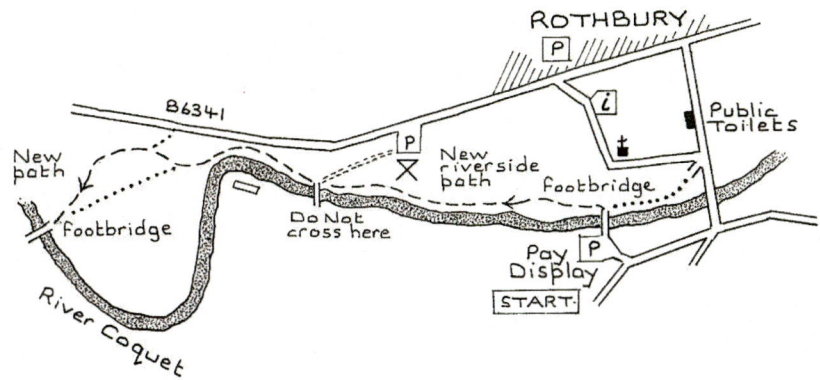

The River Coquet, named in the 7th century Ravenna Cosmography as Coc-coveda, and also mentioned by Bede in his 'Life of St.Cuthbert'.

OVER TO GREAT TOSSON

Over the footbridge and looking to your right, the long 'green' straight track to the sharp left turn at the sheep pen. There is no other way to go. Look for the old bench seat along here HOWARD + PEG, and on the hill to the right of the first house, a concrete pillbox. At Tosson Mill House, just beyond the entrance, a Victorian letterbox built into the wall.

At the road junction, turn left, and a very short way along, take the road on the right up to Great Tosson. The signpost here reads Great Tosson ½ mile - Lordenshaws 2½ miles. This road is hedged on both sides.

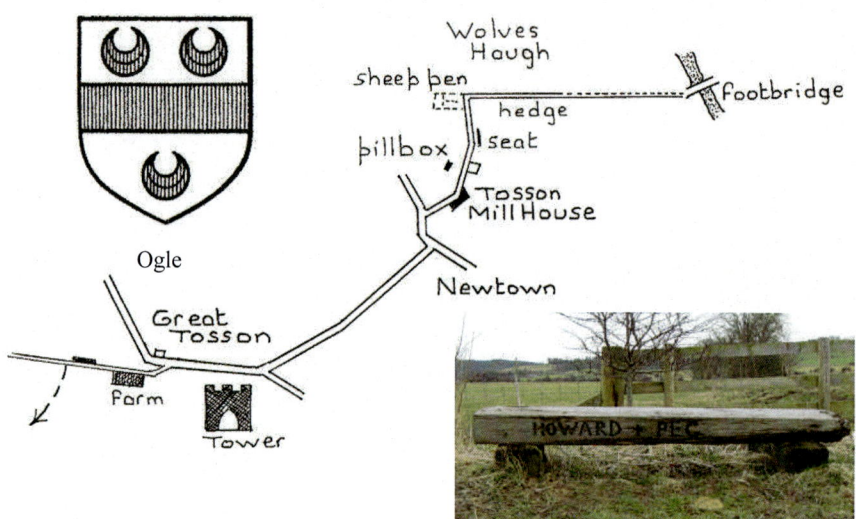

Ogle

Wolves Haugh

sheep pen

footbridge

billbox

hedge

seat

Tosson Mill House

Newtown

Great Tosson

Farm

Tower

HOWARD ➝ PEG

The long 'green' straight track.

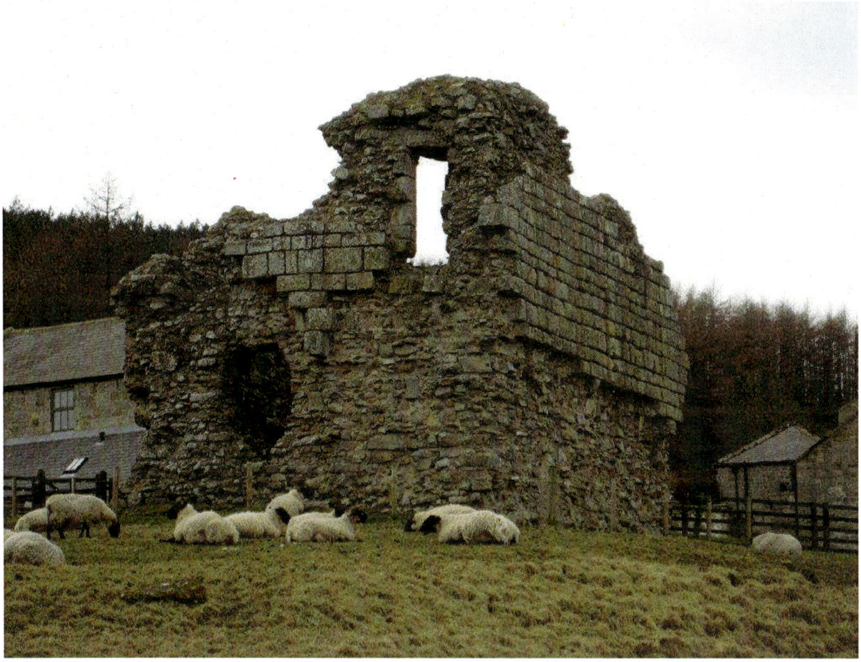

Great Tosson Tower.

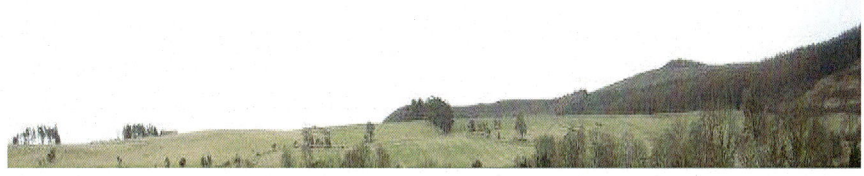

Tossan 1205, possibly 'lookout stone' long before the tower was built by the Ogle's in the 15th century as one of a defensive line of towers and castles along the Coquet Valley in a dangerous Borderland. A survey of Border Towns carried out in the reign of Henry VIII records 'At Great Tosson is a tower of lorde Ogle's Inherytance, not in good rep'ac'ons'.

At the end of the village bear left on the track along the side of the farm to reach a left stile and signpost – Public Footpath – Tosson Burgh Hill Fort ¼ - Simonside 1¼.

Left stile and signpost.

UP THROUGH THE WOODS

Up the hill, shortly through a wooden gate, continue to climb the grassy path in a well defined direction, patches of gorse, and ahead to the left, dark pines. Some great views of Coquetdale from here and you can still see Rothbury in the far distance.

Burgh Hill and you begin to notice grooved grass 'dips' and 'rounded mounds', the outer perimeter of the ancient hill fort probably dating from sometime after 600BC in the Early Iron Age. Take a short signposted detour to stand on the highest point of the hill, in prehistory where now only sheep graze and birds sing.

Above. Up the hill. Below. Through a wooden gate, and Burgh Hill

Back on route, continue on the grassy path with the forest wall on your left. This winds around and soon takes you over a stile by a field gate, then a stepped stile over a drystone wall. A short way ahead, the small gate into the forest and a wide forest track. Turn right and almost immediately look for the path on your left leading up through the forest.

Above. The forest path. Below. Straight over ahead.

The very well worn path starts to climb gently, gradually getting steeper, then levels to meet another wide forest track, continue straight over ahead. From here the path is quite stony.

The ascent is not difficult, nor is it very long. You cannot get lost since there is only one way to go.

Out in the open you can take any map marked route to the base of Simonside though the waymarked path to your left through the heather is the preferred option.

The signpost left.

SIMONSIDE TO THE BEACON

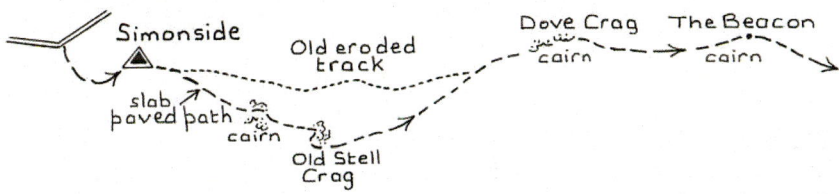

Now for the Simonside climb. It doesn't take long, it's not too steep and you'll certainly feel a sense of achievement standing on this 'mountain top'. The views are breathtaking over forest and patchwork fields. To the south in direct contrast, a seemingly endless remote landscape.

Off Simonside top pick up the new paved slab path to the cairn, good easy walking. From Old Stell Crag the slab path winds through the heather, look out for Red Grouse. Dove Crag, and a short descent to a stepped stile and along to The Beacon.

Newtown Park below was once part of a medieval deer park enclosed in the 13th century. Records record deer here in 1368, though by 1702 none left to hunt.

Simonside top.

Simonside – documented in 1279 as Simundessete.
The 16th century was a troubled time in this Borderland. In 1549 on Old Stell Crag a watch was kept on this 'beakon of Simonsyde' to warn of any Scots invasion.

Dangerous Dwarfs known as Duergar are supposed to haunt the Simonside Hills and by devious means, lure unsuspecting travellers to their doom.

MYSTERIOUS STONES

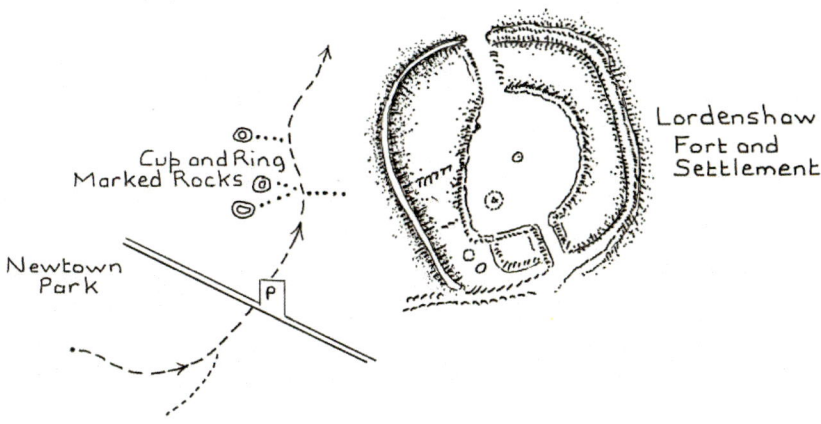

From The Beacon the rocky path, with paved slab sections, descends to the road and car park at Lordenshaw Iron Age Hill Fort. Here the signpost reads Whittondean 1 – Rothbury 2. Head straight across the car park, walk up and look up to your left to see a prominent 'metal' sign…by a rock full of Rock Art, Cup

Cup and Ring rock.

and Ring markings made by our ancestors so very long ago and whose exact purpose, despite many theories, still remains a mystery.

With the Fort and Settlement on the higher ground to your right follow the main path as it bends on its way to Whittondean.

FIELDS AND A FOLLY

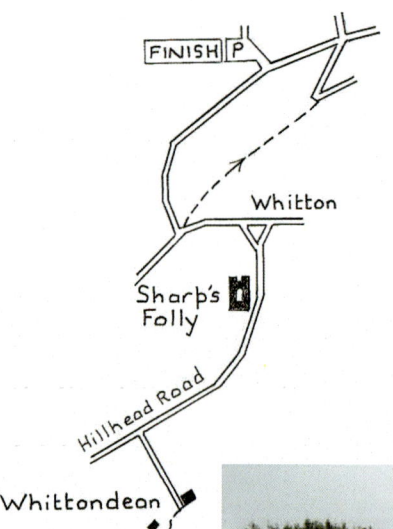

The grass path slopes downhill towards a 'cottage' in the valley. Now in the valley bottom at the pond (two ponds but one very overgrown) a wide track leads up to the left in front of the cottage to the main Whittondean House. A small gate to the left of the house leads onto the farm road from here to Hillhead Road, and a right turn to Sharp's Folly.

It's the earliest folly in the county. Look for the plaque on the wall here.

The ponds.

Sharp's Folly.

Sharp's Folly erected by Rev. Dr. Thomas Sharp Rector of Rothbury 1720-1758 'For the relief of unemployment amongst local stonemasons and use as an Observatory'.

The road continues into Whitton, then left downhill to a road junction.

On your immediate left, the entrance to Whitton Tower, with a Victorian letterbox set into the wall. The tower was originally built around 1386 by Thomas De Umfraville having subsequently served as Rothbury Rectory and then a Children's Convalescent Home. It's not visible from the road and now a private residence not open to the public.

At the road junction and directly opposite the entrance to the tower, it's through a small gate and over the sloping field to meet the road downhill to the bridge over the Coquet, then left and back along to the car park…and now you can claim to have walked The Rothbury Round…and be a

Rothbury Rounder.

GRID REFERENCES

Cowhaugh Car Park	057 015
Footbridge	043 013
Great Tosson	028 005
Simonside	024 987
The Beacon	046 986
Car Park	052 988
Hillhead Road	053 003
Cowhaugh Car Park	057 015

FGS GRADING

Grading is F6 [D1, N1, T1, R1, H2]

Distance	1	6 – 12 miles
Navigation	1	Basic navigation skills needed
Terrain	1	50 – 75% on graded track or path 25 – 50% off track
Remoteness	1	Countryside in fairly close proximity to habitation – at least 80% of the route within 2 miles
Height	2	Over 125 ft per mile

WALK 2: ROTHBURY TERRACES
Lord Armstrong's Carriageway

Walk a nineteenth century carriageway through woods and over high level moorland, with breathtaking views of Coquetdale and the Cheviot Hills.

GRADE: T4[D0, N1, T1, R1, H1] **DISTANCE:** 5.75 miles (9.2 km)
START: Cowhaugh Car Park **TIME:** 3 - 4 hours
GRID: NU 057 015 **MAP:** 332 Alnwick & Amble

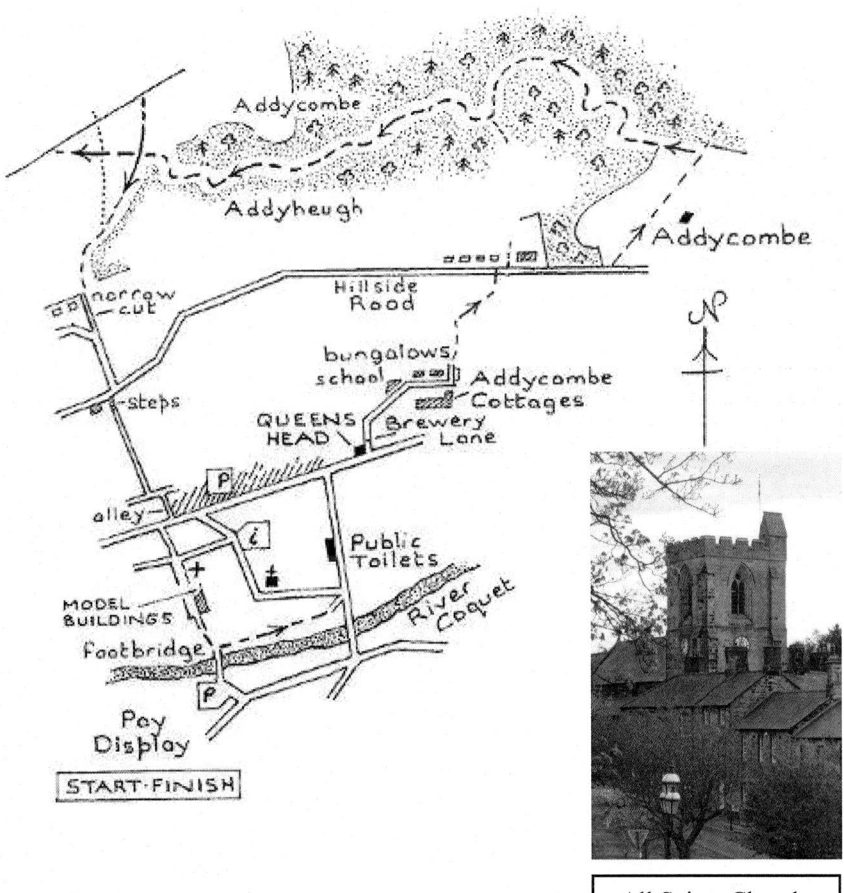

All Saints Church.

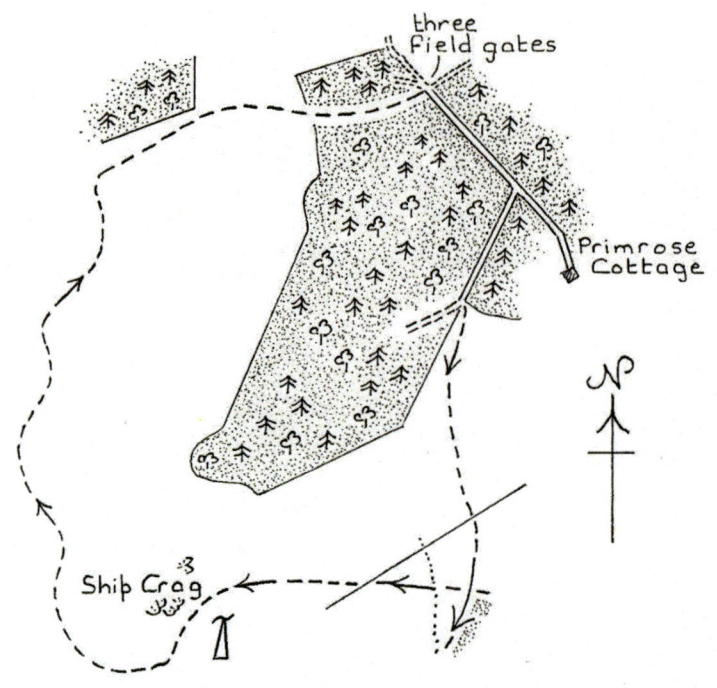

Bridge over the River Coquet.

UP FROM ROTHBURY

From the Car Park turn right over the footbridge, along to the main road bridge, then into town and The Queens Head Hotel. At the hotel corner, turn left up Brewery Lane and bear right uphill to the school and impressive long line of Addycombe Cottages, built in 1873 by Lord Armstrong of Cragside for retired staff who had worked in his household.

The road bends around to the right, with bungalows on your left. Just past the bungalows, turn left up a short gravel track to a small gate.

Above. Addycombe Cottages. Small gate. Below. From the fenced path.

From the gate, a narrow fenced path leads up to Hillside Road. Look back to see the school with Simonside clearly visible in the far distance. At Hillside Road, turn right, ignoring the first footpath on your left. Continue along past Addycombe Villa into a wide unsurfaced track with a wood on your left and just beyond the wood look for the stepped stile on your left to a 'green path' leading diagonally up over the fields. The building you see on your right is Addycombe. At the top of the fields, a kissing gate, and Lord Armstrong's Carriageway along Rothbury Terraces. The Carriageway was laid out by the first Lord Armstrong as a scenic circular drive.

Above. The stepped stile. Below. Kissing gate at the Carriageway.

THE CARRIAGEWAY ALONG THE TERRACES

Turn left at the carriageway kissing gate and beech wood, with views of Rothbury below. The carriageway looks more like a wide track and shortly comes to a fork. Ignore the left fork downhill and continue on the main right track uphill. Then along the track, a distinctive flat rock outcrop topped with a large boulder. Bird feeders hang on the trees here.

Continue on to a kissing gate and field gate, where the woods end and the open moorland begins. The visual contrast is dramatic. Still on the wide track, it's up to the 'mast' by Ship Crag for breathtaking views. The track then winds over

Continue uphill.

open moorland in this inspirational remote place, eventually to three field gates.

The flat rock outcrop.

Kissing gate and field gate

WOODS AND MOORLAND

At the three field gates turn right past the 'forest sign', then down the track to the first right turn, signposted -Public Footpath-Rothbury 1¼. Just beyond the track barrier under large shaded beeches, an old flatbed trailer long since left to rust away in an idyllic location. The track carries on to a corner and bears right. Look very carefully here for the gate and stile on your left to follow a well defined path out into open moorland, then gradually up and back to the carriageway track which you'll recognize as having walked along earlier.

Forest sign.

The track barrier.

The old flatbed trailer.

DOWN TO ROTHBURY

At the carriageway track continue straight over through the trees and down a rocky path to a stile and narrow cut. At the bottom of the 'cut' follow the road downhill to Hillside Road. Turn right here and immediately look diagonally across the road to an opening in the wall and steps down to a well surfaced narrow path between houses to reach a minor road. Turn left and a very short way along look for the alley on your right (known locally as the Nick). Down here and you're back into Rothbury. Cross over to The United Reformed Church into a lane and a terrace named Model Buildings, built 1891 as state of the art workers houses, then a narrow path and over the bridge to finish your walk.

Above. Straight over the carriageway track. Below. Hillside Road.

GRID REFERENCES

Cowhaugh Car Park	057 015
Hillside Road	060 022
Path/track junction	065 025
Track/path junction	054 025
Track junction	055 038
Path/track junction	054 025
Cowhaugh Car Park	057 015

FGS GRADING

Grading is T4 [D0, N1, T1, R1, H1]

Distance	0	Up to 6 miles
Navigation	1	Basic navigation skills needed
Terrain	1	50 – 75% on graded track or path 25 – 50% off track
Remoteness	1	Countryside in fairly close proximity to habitation – at least 80% of the route within 2 miles
Height	1	Over 100 ft per mile

WALK 3: DARDEN LOUGH

Through heather moorland to a 'secret lake' and one of the best viewpoints in Coquetdale.

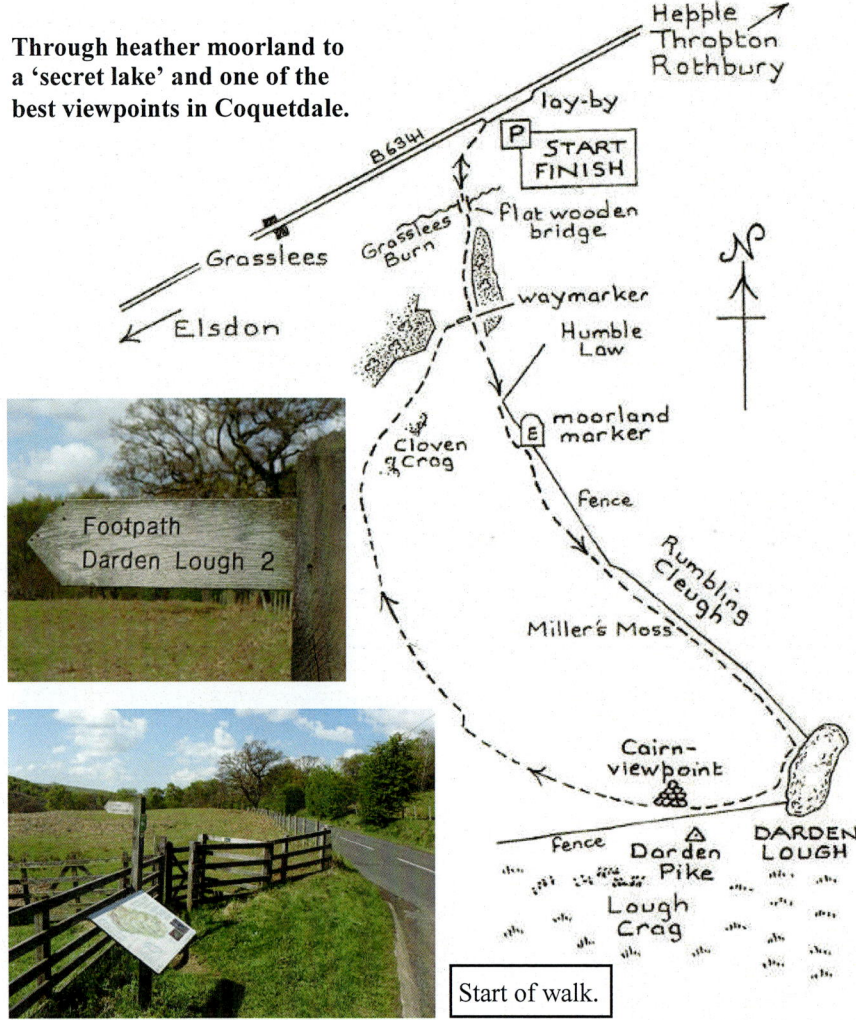

Start of walk.

From Hepple you'll come to a well signposted Northumberland National Park Car Park and Picnic Area on your right. Continue on towards Grasslees for about 1¼ miles looking carefully for the layby on your left, which is not signposted. There's an Information Board here and a waymarker-Footpath-Darden Lough 2. This is the start of the walk.

GRADE: F6 [D0, N1, T2, R1, H2]   **DISTANCE:** 4.5 miles/7.24 km
START: At layby ½ mile before Grasslees   **TIME:** 3-3½ hours
GRID: NY 959 981   **MAP:** OL42 Kielder Water & Forest

From the kissing gate a grassy path leads diagonally over the field and down to a flat wooden bridge over Grasslees Burn. Ahead the track then climbs gently uphill to a 'low' waymarker -Waymarked Footpath Circuit - Via Darden Lough – Please Keep To The Path. From this point the walk can be done in either direction. The preferred route is definitely straight ahead.

Flat wooden bridge.

Low waymarker.

Looking back to start of walk.

Path marker post.

The path through the heather is well defined with marker posts and dips down over a narrow stream, then winds up to the right and you begin to realize you're in a remote wild place, so far away from the rush of a modern world. Continue up with the long fence line on your left and where the path comes close to the fence look for the moorland marker stone, incised with the letter 'E'. On the opposite side, the letter 'T'.

On the path .

Moorland marker.

Up towards the skyline the narrow path is still well defined though rough in places, and the heather gets higher. Keep looking for the marker posts.

Darden Lough.

Over a flat squelchy area to the Lough. It's bigger than you would first imagine, it's no small pool, it's a Lake. From the Lough follow the path uphill to the Cairn viewpoint, to sit in this naturally towered place for one of the best Coquetdale visuals in every direction.

The Cairn viewpoint.

From the Cairn an obvious path with marker posts makes for an enjoyable descent with continuous opportunities to take in more views. Back at the 'low' waymarker retrace the path to the lay-by to finish.

GRID REFERENCES

Layby	959 981
Path junction	959 977
Darden Lough	970 957
Path junction	959 977
Layby	959 981

FGS GRADING

Grading is F6 [D0, N1, T2, R1, H2]

Distance	0	Up to 6 miles
Navigation	1	Basic navigation skills needed
Terrain	2	25 -50% on graded track or path 50 – 75% off track
Remoteness	1	Countryside in fairly close proximity to habitation – at least 80% of the route within 2 miles
Height	2	Over 125 ft per mile

WALK 4: ROTHBURY- FIELDS, FOREST and MOOR

Experience three very different Coquetdale landscapes.

GRADE: T4 [D1, N1, T1, R1, H0]   **DISTANCE:** 8.4 miles / 13.5 km
START: Cowhaugh Car Park   **TIME:** 4 - 5 hours.
GRID: NU O57 015   **MAP:** OL42 Kielder Water & Forest

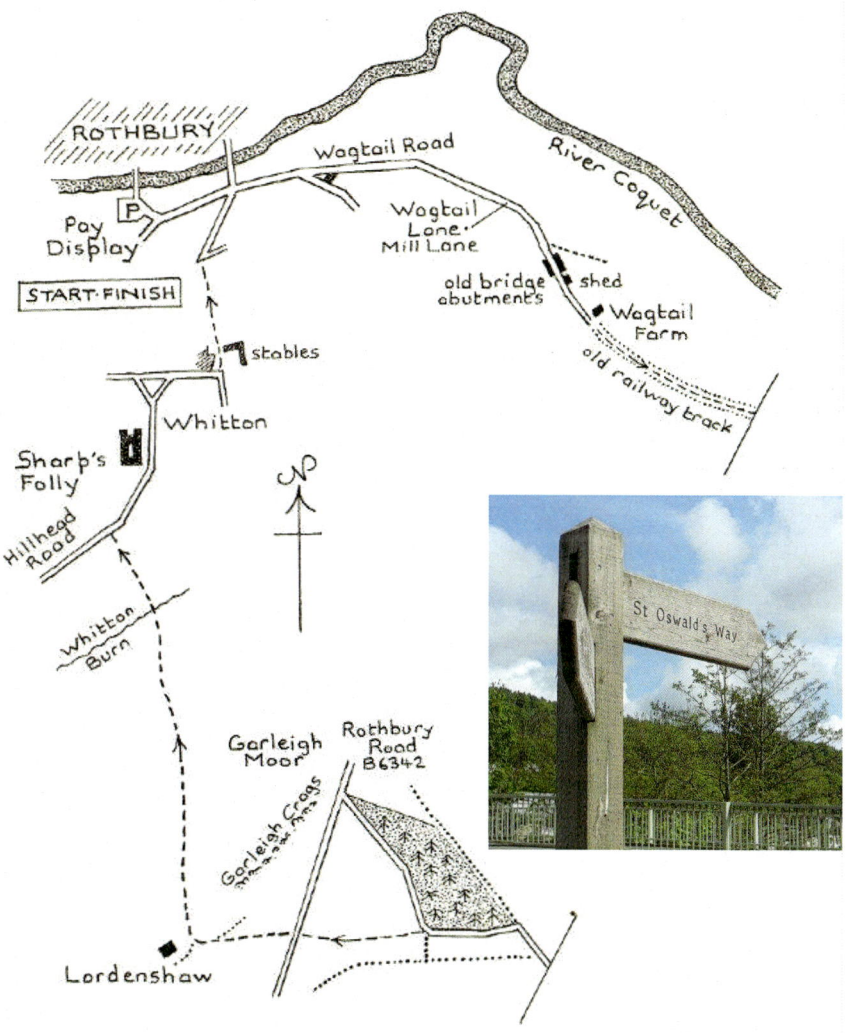

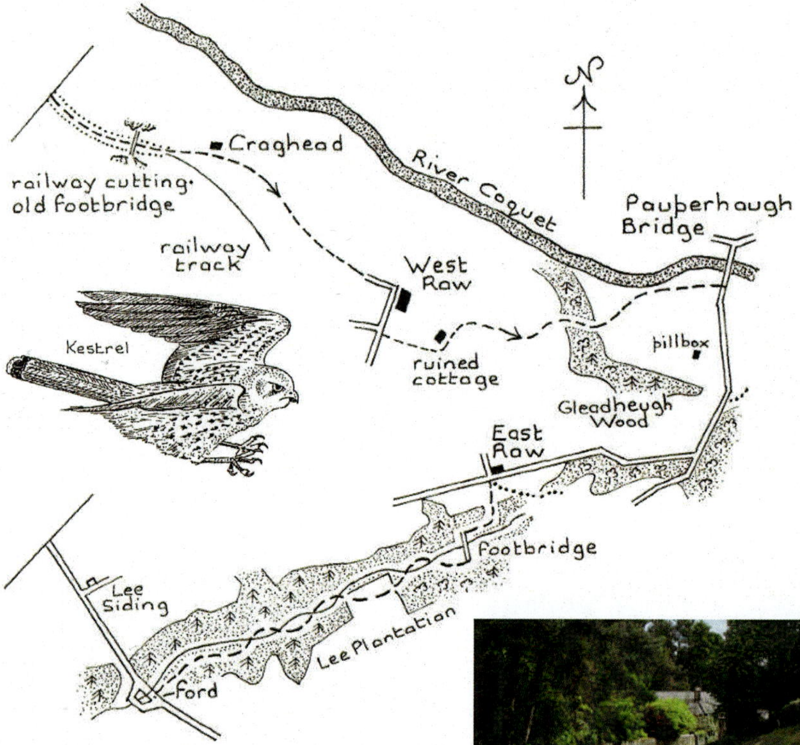

Map labels:
- Craghead
- railway cutting·
- old footbridge
- railway track
- River Coquet
- N
- Pauperhaugh Bridge
- West Row
- ruined cottage
- pillbox
- Kestrel
- Gleadheugh Wood
- East Row
- footbridge
- Lee Siding
- Lee Plantation
- Ford

LANE, TRACKS AND FIELDS

Turn left out of the Car Park and follow the path along to the main road bridge.
A waymarker here indicates St Oswald's Way, straight ahead uphill. Continue uphill until the road curves to the right, here another road leads off left. There's a St Oswald's Way waymarker and house facing across the junction and a sign, WAGTAIL ROAD-LEADING TO WAGTAIL LANE. Take this road which becomes a country lane, shown on the OS Map as Mill Lane, though also known as Wagtail Lane leading to Wagtail Farm.

Above. Ahead uphill.
Below. Along Wagtail Road.

ST OSWALD'S WAY, a long distance path connecting Holy Island on the Northumbrian Coast to Heavenfield in Hadrian's Wall Country. King Oswald re-introduced Christianity to Northumbria in the 7th century and is recorded in Bede's 'History of the English Church and People'. This part of the walk follows the course of St Oswald's Way to just up from Pauperhaugh Bridge.

Down to old bridge abutments, follow the lane through the abutments past a little shed on your left to reach Wagtail Farm and a stile by a metal field gate. You're now on the course of an old railway track. Along the track a narrow 'cutting' with a sheer rock face on either side and old broken footbridge above. Then through a wooden fieldgate to look very carefully for a stile on your left beside a metal fieldgate. Here the walk leaves the railway track and leads diagonally across the field to Craghead, derelict and left to the ravages of time in this

Above. Old bridge abutments.
Below. The narrow cutting.

Above. Old railway track.
Below. Over to Craghead.

place where only sheep now graze.

From Craghead, well defined field paths and a hedged track to West Raw. Follow the track around to the right to reach the corner of a road and immediately ahead to your left look for the waymarker – Public Footpath – Pauperhaugh ¾. The grassy track leads to a ruined cottage. The way then bends right over a field with no obvious path. Take an almost straight line towards the trees. As you walk across the field you're unlikely to see the gate into the woods until you are near the trees. The path through this short section of woods slopes down to fields by the River Coquet and along to Pauperhaugh Bridge, 1862.

| Above. Right, around West Raw. Below. Gate into woods. | Above. To the ruined cottage. Below. Pauperhaugh Bridge. |

IN THE FOREST

Turn right at Pauperhaugh Bridge and the short quiet country road to East Raw. At the T-junction here a road sign reads 'Brinkburn Station'. Beside this sign a wooden gate and waymarker-Public Footpath-The Lee 1¼-Embleton Terrace ¾. Take the direction of the waymarker over the field into the forest, down to the footbridge and the path on your right following the forest burn. The path criss-crosses the burn no less than six times though stepping stones make this relatively easy. The way through the woods will certainly prove to be a well remembered part of this walk. At the ford, a wide wooden bridge avoids the need to get your feet wet. It's then up the road to Lee Siding.

| Above. To the forest. Below. Across the burn. | Above. Over the footbridge. Below. The ford. |

OVER THE MOOR

Follow the road from Lee Siding to the forest corner and waymarker-Public Footpath-Rothbury Road-(B6342) ½-then over the fields past a pile of large stones. From the Rothbury Road, it's straight over to Lordenshaw and a right turn up to Garleigh Moor. You're now in a wild open expanse on a gradually climbing rough path through heather, to reach the top of the moor and a Rothbury view with Sharp's Folly in the middle distance. The path descends to Whitton Burn and up over fields to Hillhead Road and past Sharp's Folly into Whitton.

Pile of large stones.

Rothbury view.

Where the road forks at Whitton, take the right fork, then right again to the corner where the road bends right. At this corner look for the stables on your left. Between the stables and house in the left corner a narrow 'cutting' facing a low wall. It's through here to immediate views of Rothbury and over the field to the road downhill and the bridge over the Coquet, then left and back along to the Car Park.

Sharp's Folly.

Narrow 'cutting'.

GRID REFERENCES

Cowhaugh Car Park	057 015
West Raw	091 995
Pauperhaugh Bridge	101 994
East Raw	093 988
Road	079 980
Above Lordenshaw	058 985
Hillhead Road	057 005
Cowhaugh Car Park	057 015

FGS GRADING

Grading is T4 [D1, N1, T1, R1, H0]

Distance	1	6 – 12 miles
Navigation	1	Basic navigation skills needed
Terrain	1	50 – 75% on graded track or path 25 – 50% off track
Remoteness	1	Countryside in fairly close proximity to habitation – at least 80% of the route within 2 miles
Height	0	Less than 100 ft per mile

WALK 5: CARTINGTON CASTLE

Discover a new walking circular and a 'medieval' castle in this little known corner of Coquetdate

GRADE: T6 [D1, N1, T1, R1, H2]
START: By the road bridge
GRID: NU 030 022

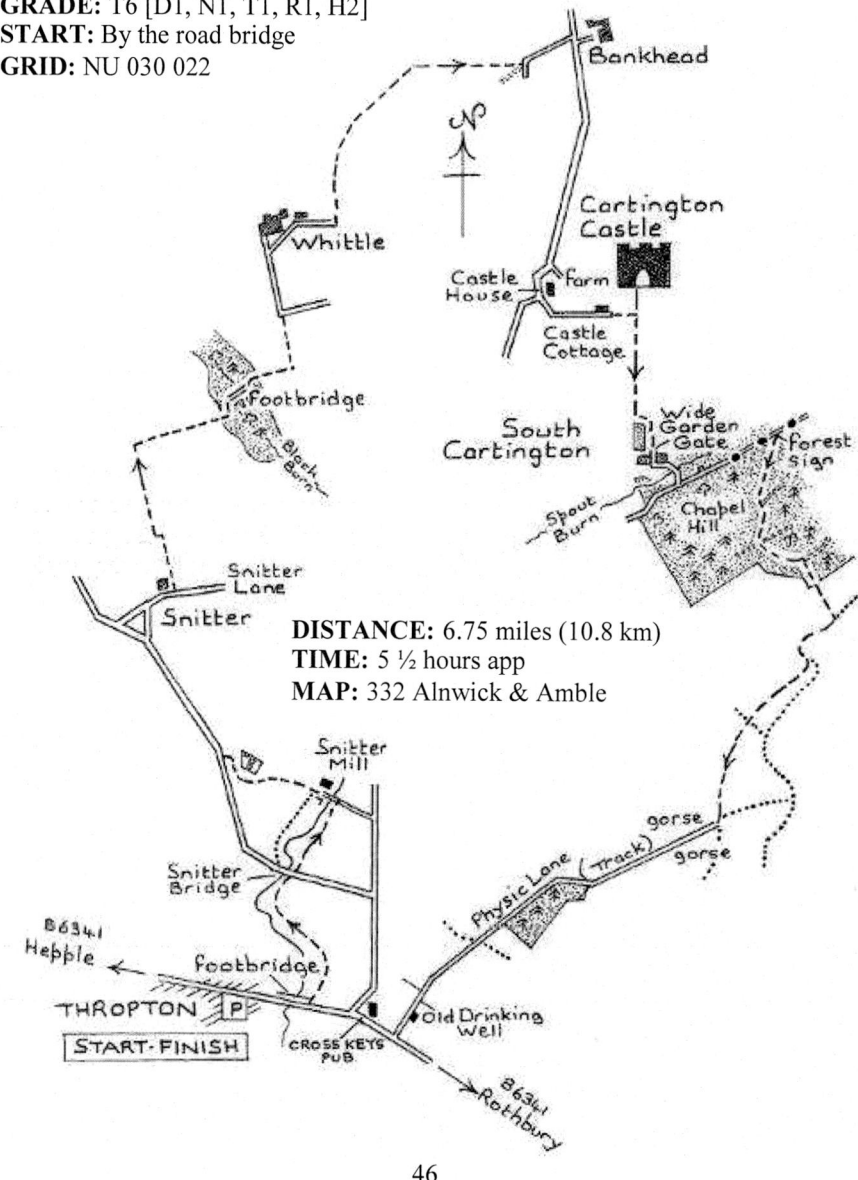

DISTANCE: 6.75 miles (10.8 km)
TIME: 5 ½ hours app
MAP: 332 Alnwick & Amble

THROPTON TO SNITTER

Start by the white railings at the road bridge. You won't be able to see it from the road but there's a footbridge over the river here, to a waymarker-Public Footpath-Snitter Bridge ½. At Snitter Bridge, look directly across the road for a stile and waymarker-Public Footpath, over the field to Snitter Mill. Don't forget to look back for the distant Simonside views.

Thropton footbridge.

Snitter Bridge.

Passed the Mill House and stone barn, through a wooden fieldgate to a fenced environmental processing area. The OS map shows the path going through this area...no. Follow the fence around to the left, then right to a wooden gate in a corner between a post and rail fence and hedge. It's then a short country road into Snitter, a well kept 'pretty little village'.

Through Snitter Mill.

To Snitter road.

Thropton – Tropton 1177 – 'Estate with an outlying farmstead or hamlet'
Snitter – Snitere 1176 – 'Possibly a weather beaten place'

47

TO BANKHEAD AND CARTINGTON

At the north end of the village, a road junction and corner cottage. Take the right fork passed the cottage to Snitter Lane, and immediately after the big house on the left look for the waymarker-Footpath-Whittle 1-Bankhead 2. The path across the fields is not clearly defined, but directionally easy to follow to metal field gates and a 'left' and 'right' bend, then straight ahead to a wooden fieldgate hinged on a stone post.

Waymarker to Whittle and Bankhead.

Fieldgate and stone post.

Through the fieldgate, turn right and down the edge of the field to a kissing gate into the wood and a footbridge over the Black Burn. From the kissing gate at the opposite side of the wood, walk directly up the field to a fence line where a marker post indicates a left turn, along the fence line to another kissing gate and the road into Whittle.

Over the Black Burn.

Up to the fence line.

The farmhouse at Whittle is very unusual, just a plain building seen from the road but with a unique feature when you actually reach it. An end elevation has been added to look like an old tower, crenellated with elaborate 'blanked' windows, all 19th century mock gothic. Someone wanted their house here to be more visually attractive and the combination of two completely different architectural styles is certainly an eye-catcher.

From Whittle, turn right down the track which bears left and along to an obvious cross track. Ignore the cross track and carry straight on to a metal fieldgate, then right up to Bankhead and a short road walk into Cartington. Follow the road passed the farm entrance and around to Castle House with its decorative topiary. Where the road curves right downhill turn left and along to Castle Cottage and a stile by a metal fieldgate. From this corner….Cartington Castle.

| Above. Whittle.
Below. Castle House Topiary. | Above. Turn right to Bankhead.
Below. Castle Cottage stile. |

CARTINGTON CASTLE

Cartington

Radcliffe   Widdrington   Charlton

Cartington-Cretenden 1220-Probably 'hill associated with a man called Certa' The Manor was granted by Henry II in 1154 to his Forester, Ralph Fitz-Main whose descendants seem to have held the post until the early 14th century. Many others however, held lands in Cartington, including Richard Frebern de Kertinden in 1234 and John de Kertington in 1278.

A John de Cartington is recorded as having held the 'Turris de Kartyngton' in 1415 and in 1441 licence to crenellate-Royal permission to add battlements and fortify-was granted and Cartington became an impressive hall-house.

By the end of the 15th century the Manor had passed through marriage to the Radcliffes. On 16th November 1515, Princess Margaret, sister of Henry VIII stayed here after the birth of her daughter at Harbottle Castle… 'a place of Sir Edward Radcliffe's called Cartington, where she remained four days…' and in 1541 Cartington was described as 'a good fortresse of twoo toures and other strange stone houses'. The castle again passed through marriage and inheritance to the Widdringtons, and to Sir Edward Widdrington, a Royalist whose estates were forfeited during the Civil War and then given back to him after the Restoration of Charles II in 1660.

Once more through marriage Cartington passed to the Charltons of Hesleyside and subsequently to one Jack Talbot who lost it when he supported the 1715 Jacobite Rebellion.

The property was eventually purchased by Giles Alcock, a Newcastle Merchant, then a family known as the Becks, after which it seems nothing was done to avoid the castle becoming an uninhabitable ruin.

'The portal now admits the straggling sheep,
The long grass waves about the ruin'd keep;
The playful breezes whistle thro' each cell,
Where bats and moping owls sole tenants dwell'

In 1883 Lord Armstrong of Cragside bought Cartington and instigated restoration work, though more romantically visual than historically correct.

There is every expectation this 'key Northumbrian Castle' will be properly restored.

CARTINGTON TO THROPTON

There's no visible path from here. Follow the fence line down the fields and around the outside of the woods at the bottom of the hill to a wide metal 'garden gate' into South Cartington. On the road out look for the old Victorian street lights between the bridge and the T-junction. Turn left at this junction up to a waymarker-Public Footpath-Rothbury 1¾, and a big 'Blue Mill' forest sign. A gradual forest climb on a wide track curves up to moorland on the right. Look very carefully for a marker post and a right turn to a stepped stile over a dry stone wall.

Above. Gate into South Cartington.
Below. Turn right.

Above. Forest sign.
Below. Stepped stile.

Now out on the open moor to a marker post to follow the 'Rothbury Terraces' track right, a very short distance along to a wide defined grassy path that curves off to the right (no waymarkers). The grassy path descends to a wooden field gate on the right and the narrow path which winds down through a vast expanse of gorse to a track, Physic Lane and houses. As you walk down here look for the Old Drinking Well on the left…. DRINK REST AND BE THANKFULL

At the bottom of the bank, the main 'Rothbury Road'. Turn right to the Cross Keys Pub where you can opt for a well deserved pause, then back into Thropton.

Above. Moorland marker post.
Below. Field gate and 'gorse' path.

Above. Right, on grassy path.
Below. Old Drinking Well.

GRID REFERENCES

Thropton	030 022
Snitter	025 034
Whittle	026 048
Bankhead	036 057
Road/track junction	037 045
Track junction	044 041
Stile	045 035
Gate	044 027
Thropton	030 022

FGS GRADING

Grading is T6 [D1, N1, T1, R1, H2]

Distance	1	6 – 12 miles
Navigation	1	Basic navigation skills needed
Terrain	1	50 – 75% on graded track or path 25 – 50% off track
Remoteness	1	Countryside in fairly close proximity to habitation – at least 80% of the route within 2 miles
Height	2	Over 125 ft per mile

WALK 6: COPPER SNOUT and CLENNELL STREET

Remote rolling hills and an ancient drove road

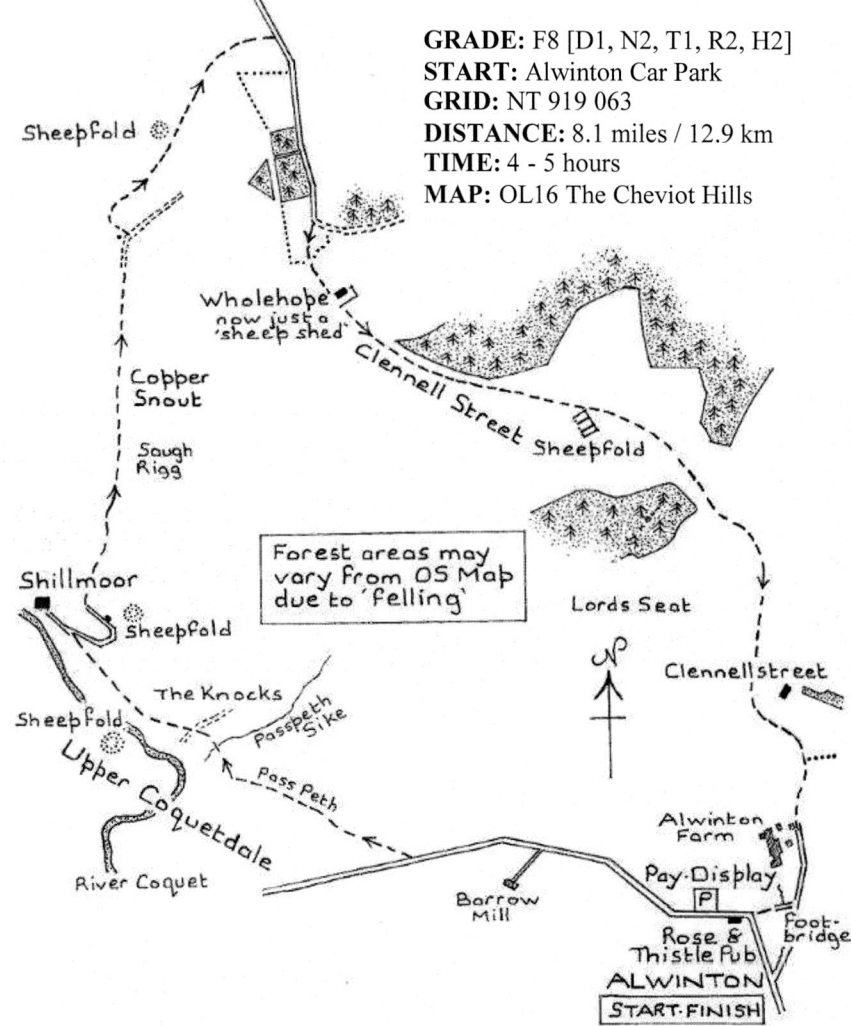

GRADE: F8 [D1, N2, T1, R2, H2]
START: Alwinton Car Park
GRID: NT 919 063
DISTANCE: 8.1 miles / 12.9 km
TIME: 4 - 5 hours
MAP: OL16 The Cheviot Hills

Sheepfold

Wholehope
now just a
'sheep shed'

Clennell Street Sheepfold

Copper
Snout

Sough
Rigg

Forest areas may
vary from OS Map
due to 'felling'

Lords Seat

Shillmoor

Sheepfold

The Knocks

Passpeth Sike

Clennell street

Sheepfold

Upper Coquetdale

Pass Peth

Alwinton
Farm

Pay Display

River Coquet

Borrow
Mill

Rose &
Thistle Pub

Foot-
bridge

ALWINTON

START·FINISH

Alwinton (Allenton), Alwenton, 1242, 'Farmstead or village on the River Alwin'. Walter Scott stayed at the Rose and Thistle here in 1817 whilst researching 'Rob Roy'.

ALWINTON TO CLENNELL STREET

From the Northumberland National Park Car Park, turn right and follow the road gradually uphill to reach a small field gate and waymarker-Public Bridle-way-Shillmoor 1¾.

The Car Park.

Gate and waymarker.

A well defined 'grassy' path gently climbs Pass Peth, through two small gates to a farm track curving away to the right. Ignore this track and continue straight up ahead on the less obvious grassy path to fine views of a twisting River Coquet, then a short descent to the valley bottom and across Passpeth Sike to follow the path above the river towards Shillmoor. Look for the circular dry-stone sheep-fold on the opposite bank of the river, known in Northumberland as a 'stell'.

The River Coquet.

Sheepfold.

The path joins a wide track with Shillmoor Farm immediately in front. Take a sharp right turn here, away from the farm and up the wide 'gravel' track which winds round to a circular dry-stone sheepfold and small 'breeze-block' hut, then the open expanse and remote rolling hills of Saugh Rigg and Copper Snout – enjoy the inspiration of just being here.

Turn right.

Copper Snout.

The track climbs to a right turn by a marker post and small stone boulder. Do not continue along the wide track. Turn left at this marker post up the grassy slope which curves right over the ridge of the hill and up to another circular dry-stone sheepfold, then over a 'sometimes boggy bit' to reach Clennell Street.

Left, up grassy slope.

Over to Clennell Street.

CLENNELL STREET

The ancient drove road over the English-Scottish Border, once known as 'Ermspeth'….Eagles Path.

Turn right on Clennell Street noting forest detail due to felling will vary from that shown on OS Maps. After a short distance the wide track (road) curves left at a corner. Look for the marker post on the right, and in front in the near distance, a very distinctive 'shed', all that remains of Wholehope.

Wholehope – The house which was once here opened as a Youth Hostel in April 1949 and closed around 1965. The building was demolished in the 1970's.

Take the path right over to Wholehope, and continue down to a metal field gate. Look for the boundary stone marker to the right of the gate. Follow the path along the forest edge to fenced sheepfold pens, then ahead to the crest of the hill and diagonally right downhill towards another forest plantation. Near the corner of this plantation, a wide field gate and Clennell Street continuing uphill, then down into Alwinton on a well defined way.

| Above. Over to Wholehope. Below. Boundary stone. | Above. Wholehope. Below. Into Alwinton. |

GRID REFERENCES

Alwinton	919 063
Road/path junction	906 065
Path/track junction	887 076
Track/path junction	890 096
Clennell Street	897 106
Alwinton	919 063

FGS GRADING

Grading is F8 [D1, N2, T1, R2, H2]

Distance	1	6 – 12 miles
Navigation	2	Competent navigation skills needed
Terrain	1	50 – 75% on graded track or path 25 – 50% off track
Remoteness	2	Countryside not in close proximity to habitation – less than 20% of the route within 2 miles
Height	2	Over 125 ft per mile

WALK 7: OLD ROOKLAND and BIDDLESTONE CHAPEL

To a ruin in splendid isolation and a chapel 'in the forest'

GRADE: T6 [D1, N1, T1, R1, H2]
START: Alwinton Car Park.
GRID: NT 919 063.
DISTANCE: 6.25 miles / 10 km.
TIME: 3 - 4 hours.
MAP: OL16 The Cheviot Hills.

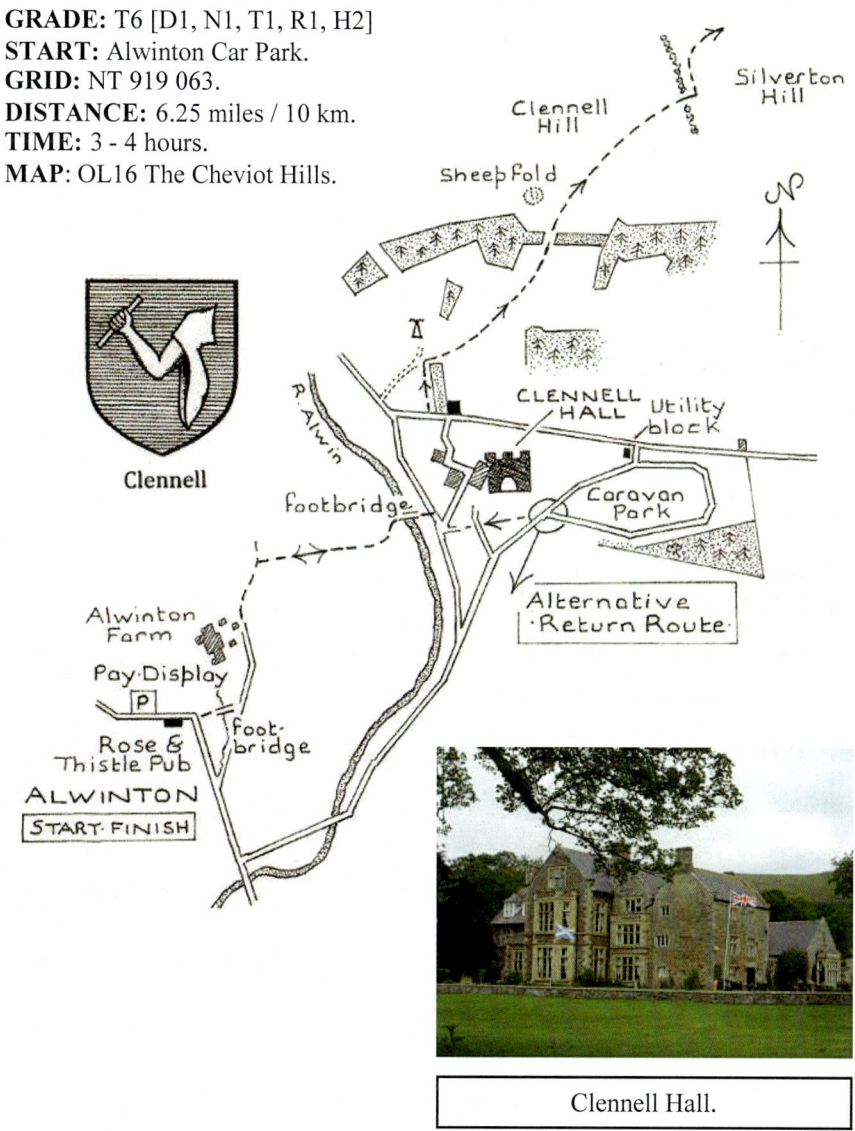

Clennell Hall.

TO OLD ROOKLAND

From the Northumberland National Park Car Park, turn left along past the Rose and Thistle pub, then directly ahead over the 'village green' and footbridge, and left up the narrow road to Alwinton Farm. Continue a short distance uphill on the wide track –Clennell Street-to a metal field gate and stile on the right.

Over the footbridge.

Metal field gate and stile.

It's over the stile and fields on a none defined way, and over the River Alwin footbridge to a waymarker-Public Bridleway-Rookland 1¾. Ignore this way-marker. You do however turn right, and almost immediately on the left a wooden field gate and cattle grid. Take this road along to Clennell Hall with the hall wall on the right.

River Alwin footbridge.

Along to Clennell Hall.

CLENNELL HALL

Documents mention Clennell as early as 1181 though the first recorded occupier was one Thomas de Clenill in 1228. It is not known what buildings stood here at this time though possibly a 'pele tower' in these dangerous Borderlands. In the Border Survey of 1541 this place was 'a lytle toure of thinherytaunce of P'cyvall Clennel'. The little tower, now part of the main house, dates from around this period, to which a two storey wing was added in 1568 and a third storey in the 1690's. What we see today mostly dates from 1895.

Follow the road, which turns left at the hall, through the farm and what was once Clennell township, and on to a junction and house by a forest plantation. Turn left, then right to the top of the plantation, then diagonally up over the fields-no marked path-towards the left of the 'rounded' Silverton Hill and a small wooden gate.

Above. Towards Silverton Hill. Below. Small wooden gate.

Next through a second wooden gate and a faint path gently up to a small wooden gate in a drystone wall with Old Rookland now in view. From here, do not be tempted to follow any obvious paths ahead but turn immediately left to follow the line of the drystone wall downhill. Where the wall bends at a corner, curve right directly to Old Rookland which you can still see in the distance. A path drops through bracken to two small wooden gates at Rookland Sike, then diagonally up through more bracken to the ruined farm.

Left. Down the wall. Right. Over Rookland Sike. Below. Old Rookland.

Old Rookland is certainly remote. It's crumbling walls seem to add an air of something you can't explain, 'in this place hidden in the hills' and last farmed by John Dagg and his family who left in 1939.

ON TO BIDDLESTONE

One of the highlights of this walk is the old track over the hills towards Biddle-stone, a wide open expanse with varied views in a rolling landscape. The track winds down. Where it forks right, continue to follow the main track left. At the road turn left and it's approximately fifteen minutes along to the Chapel.

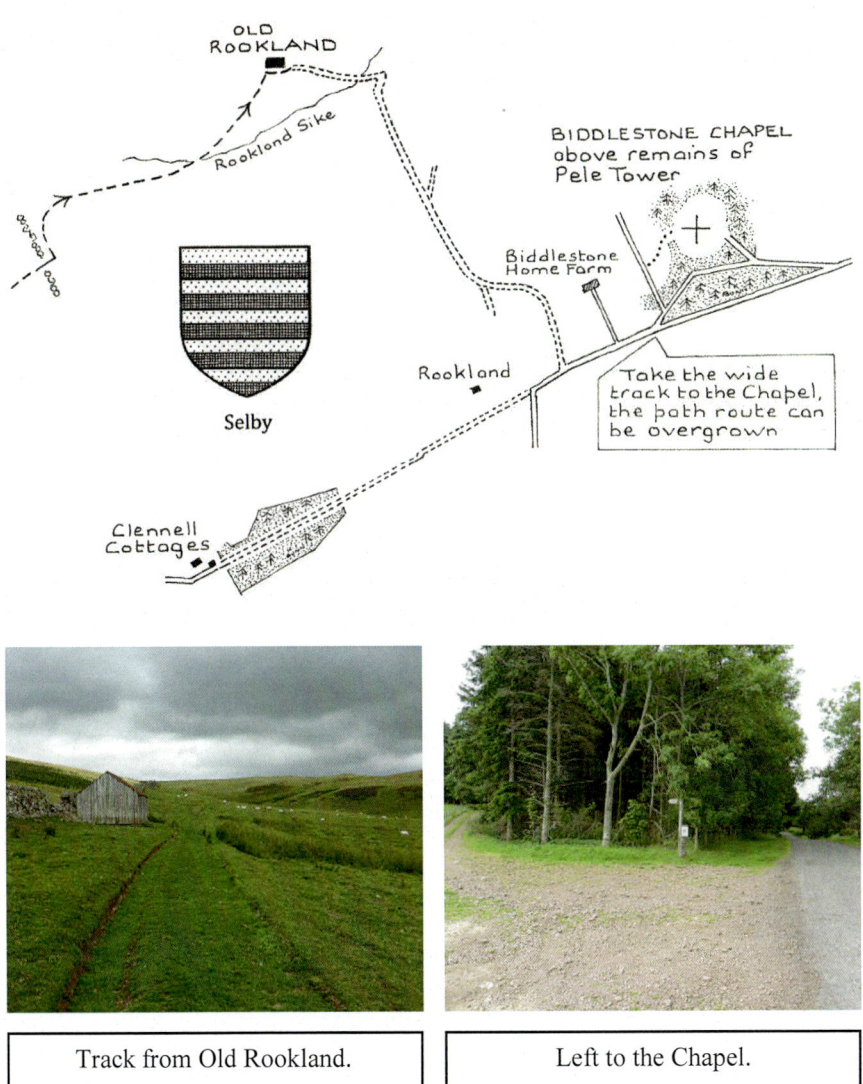

Track from Old Rookland.	Left to the Chapel.

BIDDLESTONE CHAPEL

BIDDLESTONE

The Selby's were first granted the Manor of Biddlestone in 1272. In the 14th Century they built a pele tower, mentioned in a survey of 1415 as the 'Turris de Bidilston Johannus Selby' and in 1541 said to be in 'good reparations'. In the 17th Century a house was attached to the old tower, described in 1715 as a freestone structure in the form of a cross with four wings 'middlemost tower like with battlements' and reputed to be the Osbaldiston Hall of Walter Scott's 'Rob Roy'. Around 1796 a Georgian style mansion replaced the earlier house, and in about 1820 the old pele tower was converted into a private chapel, retaining the tower base. The Selby's left Biddlestone for the last time in 1914 and although the Hall, as it was locally known, continued as a private residence and subsequently a convalescent home, it gradually deteriorated until demolished in the 1950's.

'So the Hall is gone, only to sing History's Song'.

But the Chapel remains, in a clearing surrounded by trees, visually like a holy place in a long lost legendary location.

BACK TO ALWINTON

From the Chapel it's back along the road and the track past Rookland (not to be confused with Old Rookland).

The track past Rookland.

Follow the wide 'greenway' to Clennell Cottages and continue straight on and through a wooden field gate by a small stone barn. On the left, look for a wooden field gate by a 'utility block' and permitted route through the caravan park to the main entrance.

Above. Straight ahead. Below. Through the caravan park.

From the main entrance, two options back to Alwinton, either along the riverside road, or directly across the grass by Clennell Hall perimeter hedge to the 'cattle grid' entrance to retrace the route you started on at the beginning of the walk.

GRID REFERENCES

Alwinton	919 063
Footbridge	928 070
Old Rookhope	937 088
Road	949 080
Biddleston Chapel	955 083
Road	928 070
Alwinton	919 063

FGS GRADING

Grading is T6 [D1, N1, T1, R1, H2]

Distance	1	6 – 12 miles
Navigation	1	Basic navigation skills needed
Terrain	1	50 – 75% on graded track or path 25 – 50% off track
Remoteness	1	Countryside in fairly close proximity to habitation – at least 80% of the route within 2 miles
Height	2	Over 125 ft per mile

WALK 8: HOLYSTONE

On forest trails to a Holy Well and a Waterfall

GRADE: T5 [D0, N1, T1, R1, H2]   **DISTANCE:** 4.25 miles 6.8 km.
START: Holystone Forest Enterprise Car Park   **TIME:** 3 - 3 ½ hours
GRID: NT 950 025   **MAP:** OL16 The Cheviot Hills.

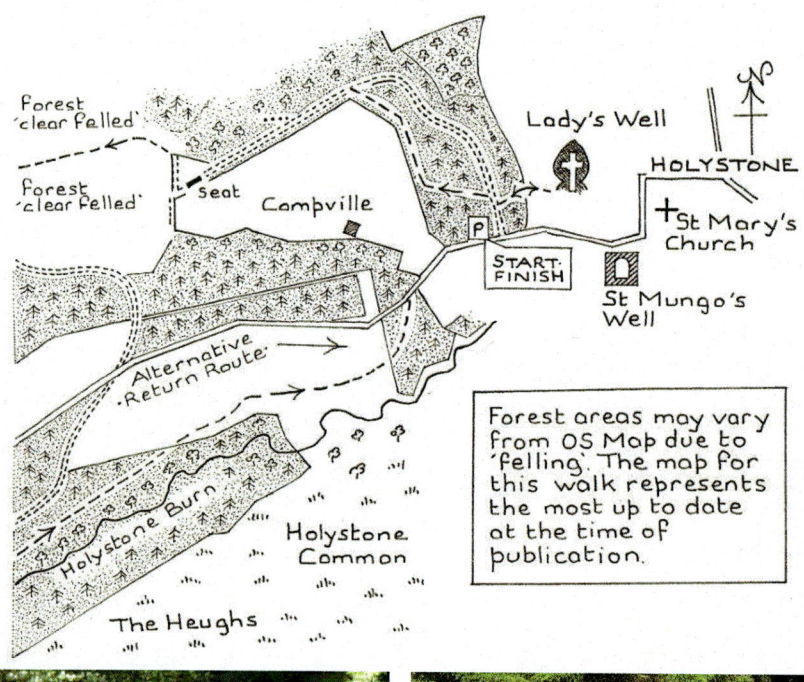

Car Park.

Information Board.

| To Ladys Well. | The Stone Altar. |

From the Car Park Information Board follow the track into the forest. A very short way ahead look for a marker post on the right-Ladys Well. Follow the path through the tree tunnel and over the field to the Well, hidden amongst tall beeches.

Ladys Well .

+ IN THIS PLACE
PAULINUS THE BISHOP
BAPTIZED
THREE THOUSAND NORTHUMBRIANS
EASTER DCXXVII +

Ladys Well, also known as St Paulinus Well and previously St Ninian's Well. The base of the standing stone cross in the centre of the enclosed clear pool records that Paulinus was here on Easter Day 627.

Tradition prevails, though it is now generally accepted, and as recorded by Bede, in his 'History of the English Church and People' that King Edwin, with all the nobility of the nation and a large number of the common sort were actually baptized by Paulinus at York on Easter Day 627.

The Ladys Well name may have originated from the Nunnery which was once in the village. The 15th century statue of Paulinus came here from Alnwick in 1780 and the stone altar is now known as the Holy Stone. There's a contemplative calm about this place, so pause awhile and reflect – there's no other location like it in all of Northumbria.

Return to the main forest track, turn right, and almost immediately on the left, a post marker and very short undefined way through the pines to reach two old stone gateposts.

Left through the pines.

72

Old stone gateposts.

A well defined path now gently climbs to a left turn and a leisurely walk by the field perimeter. Where the path forks, continue on the left path-straight ahead to a clearing and old wooden seat with open aspect views. Another Coquetdale perfect place to pause.

Wooden seat.

Single gatepost.

At the seat corner turn right, up past a single old stone gatepost. The path curves left to a vast area of clear felled forest to join a wide grass way and gravel track to a T-junction.

| Clear felled forest. | Wide grass way. |

Above. Fairy Glen.
Below. The Waterfall.

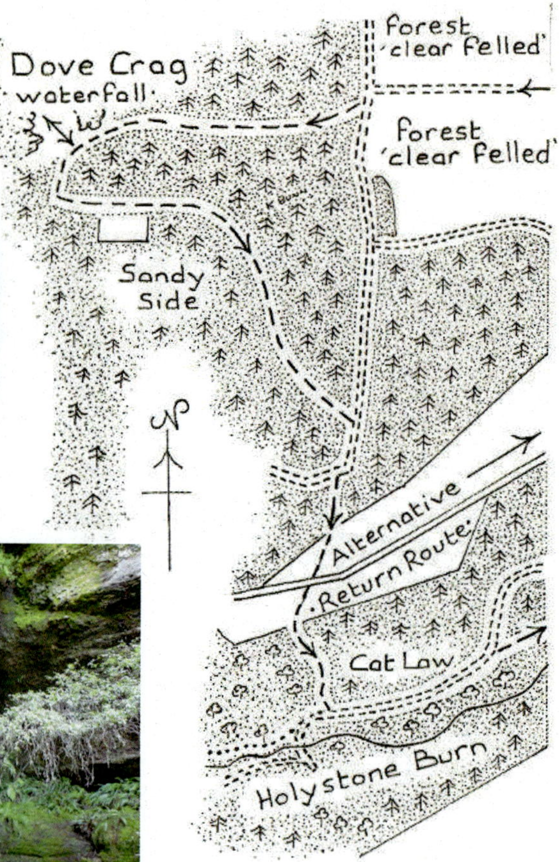

Forest 'clear felled'

Forest 'clear felled'

Dove Crag waterfall

Sandy Side

Alternative Return Route

Cat Low

Holystone Burn

74

Look directly over to the left, where a post marker indicates 'into the forest'. It doesn't look possible. Once in the forest however the wide shaded way is a truly atmospheric experience, and easy to follow to Dove Crag and the obvious high rocky outcrops. These crags are known locally as Fairy Glen, home to the little people (though no-one has ever reported seeing them). Pass the first outcrop, then look carefully on the right for the very short detour to the waterfall, where a thin single stream of water drops into a hollow rock basin. It's a surprise to the eyes, this place so few people see.

Back to the main path and an easy to follow way through the forest to a wide gravel forest road. Turn right. The road quickly curves by a marker post on the left. Take this left path through the trees and over the field to a tarmac road, once part of a Roman Road that linked their major routes at Dere Street and The Devils Causeway. You may opt to return to the start of the walk along this road.

To follow the Holystone Burn option, continue straight over the road and the path down through the woods to a wide track. Turn left at the wide track and follow this to an obvious left bend. Look for the path on the right here, noting this return route can sometimes be overgrown and wet in places.

Your walk finished, take time to see St. Mungo's Well and visit the Church.

ST MUNGO'S WELL
The Well is named
after the 6th century Scottish
evangelist though there is no
evidence of his ever having
been here. The stone structure
you now see was erected in the
19th century.

HOLYSTONE CHURCH

A Nunnery was founded on this site sometime before 1124. In 1291 there were 27 nuns here, 4 lay brothers, 3 chaplains, and a master. Despite continuous harassment from Borderland marauders this holy place seems to have survived until the Dissolution of the Monasteries in 1539. The present church of St Mary the Virgin is 19th century though part of the lower walls are probably Norman. Built into the outside wall, look for the fragments of medieval gravestones with ornamental crosses.

Above. The Church. Below. Medieval gravestones.

 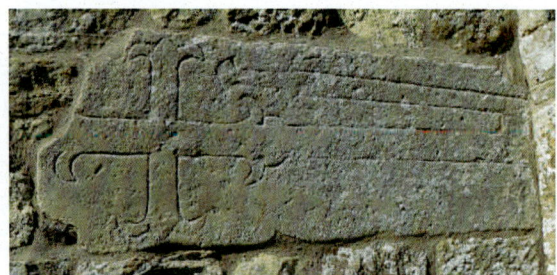

GRID REFERENCES

Car park	950 025
Lady's Well	953 029
Dove Crag	928 025
Track/path junction	934 021
Path/track junction	935 013
Car park	950 025

FGS GRADING

Grading is T5 [D0, N1, T1, R1, H2]

Distance	0	Up to 6 miles
Navigation	1	Basic navigation skills needed
Terrain	1	50 – 75% on graded track or path 25 – 50% off track
Remoteness	1	Countryside in fairly close proximity to habitation – at least 80% of the route within 2 miles
Height	2	Over 125 ft per mile

Over to Clennell. Walk 7. Old Rookland and Biddlestone Chapel.

APPENDIX

Ferguson Grading System ('FGS')

1. Introduction

The FGS has been adopted as a means of assessing the nature and severity of the various walks in this book and the abilities and equipment needed to tackle each one safely. The FGS was developed by Stuart Ferguson, a long time fell and trail runner, climber, mountaineer, mountain-biker and general outdoor enthusiast. In the opinion of Trailguides the FGS is the most accurate and comprehensive grading system for comparing off-road walking, running and mountain-biking routes anywhere in the country.

2. The System

Tables 1 & 2, set out below, are used in order to give a grading to each route. Table 1 sets out three categories of country that a route could potentially cross, together with a range of factors that would need to be considered when tackling that route. The three categories are, Trail, Fell and Mountain, and after assessing which category best fits the route, a letter, either 'T', 'F' or 'M', is allocated to that route. Where a route does not fit perfectly into one of the three categories the closest category is allocated.

Table 2 deals with five specific aspects of the route, distance, navigation, terrain, remoteness and height gain, and each one is allocated a letter, 'D', 'N', 'T', 'R', and 'H'. Each letter is also given a severity score from the range 0-3 or 0-4, in respect of distance ('D'). The higher the number, the more severe the route. The five severity scores are then added together to give an overall score. The overall score is then put with the Table 1 category letter (i.e. 'T', 'F' or 'M').

In order to show how the grading has been determined for each walk in this book, the five individual severity scores are set out, in square brackets, immediately after the actual grading. So, for example, Walk 8 Holystone has a grading of T5 [D0, N1, T1, R1, H2], indicating that it is a Trail Category walk with a total severity score of 5. This is made up of the five specific severity scores, for distance ('D'), navigation ('N'), terrain ('T'), remoteness ('R') and height gain ('H'), of 0, 1, 1, 1 and 2 respectively. The highest total severity score which can be achieved is 16 and the lowest total severity score achievable is 0.

The table which accompanies the grading at the end of each walk sets out the specific factors, extracted from Table 2, that need to be considered when tackling that particular walk.

TABLE 1

	TRAIL	FELL	MOUNTAIN
Description	Lowland and forest areas including urban, cultivated and forested locations.	Moorlands and upland areas which may include some upland cultivated and forestry areas plus possibly remote locations.	Upland and mountain areas including remote and isolated locations.
Height	Not usually above 1,000 feet but may go up to 2,500 feet	Usually above 1,000 feet, up to 2,500 feet and above.	Usually above 2,500 feet and up to 4,000 feet.
Way-marking	Usually	Limited	None
Terrain	Usually graded paths, tracks and trails but may include some off-trail	May include some graded paths, tracks and trails but mainly off-trail	Virtually all off-trail
Height gain	Limited height gain	May include considerable height gain	May include some severe height gain.
Effects of weather	Very limited effect	May be prone to sudden weather changes	Extreme weather a possibility
Navigational skills	None to basic	Basic to competent	Competent to expert
Equipment	Walking shoes/boots. Possibly waterproofs Food and drink dependant upon route.	3/4 season walking boots. Full waterproof cover. Possibly map and compass dependant upon route. Food and drink dependant upon route.	Mountain boots. Full waterproof cover. Map and compass. Food and drink
Escape Routes	Yes	Some	Some to nil

TABLE 2

Score	0	1	2	3	4
Distance	Up to 6 miles	6 – 12 miles	12 – 18 miles	18 miles +	24 miles +
Navigation	No navigation skills needed	Basic navigation skills needed	Competent navigation skills needed	Expert navigation skills needed	
Terrain	75% + on graded track or path	50 – 75% on graded track or path 25 – 50% off track	25 -50% on graded track or path 50 – 75% off track	Under 25% on graded track or path Over 75% off track	
Remoteness	Urban	Countryside in fairly close proximity to habitation – at least 80% of the route within 2 miles	Countryside not in close proximity to habitation – less than 20% of the route within 2 miles	Remote, isolated location	
Height gain	Less than 100 ft per mile	Over 100 ft per mile	Over 125 ft per mile	Over 250 ft per mile	

Notes to Table 2

Graded paths = Well established paths with a stable surface.

Escape routes = The opportunity to cut the route short and return to the start without completing the full course in the event of weather changes or unforeseen incidents.

The Author

Kenneth Bunn

Ken's 'Walking Ways' are really too numerous to list - Geneva to Nice over the Alps, The French Pyrenees, Tour of Mont Blanc, Basque Country, The Queyras, and in Italy Monte Viso - the more familiar Highlands and Islands of Scotland, The Pennine Way, Offas Dyke, Coast to Coast, Yorkshire Three Peaks, and decades of walking, in the Lake District and throughout County Durham and Northumberland.

It's been said he was born with a rucksac on his back. Uniquely Ken has also been recording and illustrating almost every walk he's ever done, and that's a lot of walks. His detailed hand drawn maps have often become definitive information with his knowledge of North Country history adding additional interest.

Only those who actually walked with Ken had access to his many personal write ups ….. until now.

Walking North East

Walking North East is the brand name for the walking publications produced by Trailguides and reflects the pride that we, as North Easterners, have in our countryside, our history and our culture.

Based in Darlington, we are a small independent publisher specialising in guidebooks centred on the North Eastern counties of England. Our target is to produce guides that are as user-friendly, easy to use and provide as much information as possible and all in an easily readable format. In essence to increase the enjoyment of the user and to showcase the very best of the great North Eastern countryside. Our series of books explores the heritage of us all and lets you see your region with new eyes, these books are written to not just take you on a walk but to investigate, explore and understand the objects, places and history that has shaped not just the countryside but also the people of this corner of England.

If you've enjoyed following the routes in this guide and want news and details of other publications that are being developed under the Walking North East label then look at the company website at **www.trailguides.co.uk**

Comments and, yes, criticisms, are always welcomed especially if you discover a change to a route. Contact us by email through the website or by post at Trailguides Limited, 35 Carmel Road South, Darlington, Co Durham DL3 8DQ.

Other walking books from Walking North East.
At the time of publication the following books are also available but with new titles being regularly added to our publication list keep checking our website.

Northumberland.
The Cheviot Hills.
Walks from Wooler.
The Hills of Upper Coquetdale.
Walks from Kirknewton.
Walks on the Wild Side: The Cheviot Hills.
Walks around Rothbury and Coquetdale.

County Durham.
Hamsterley Forest.
The Barningham Trail.
Ancient Stones.
The High Hills of Teesdale.

Walks from Stanhope.
Mid-Teesdale Walks.
Walks around Frosterley and Weardale.

North Yorkshire.
The Hills of Upper Swaledale.
Walks around Gunnerside.

Walking North East.
Visit our website and sign up to receive our free newsletter, Walking North East, dedicated to walking in North Eastern England. Full of news, views and articles relating to this the forgotten corner of England.

Acknowledgements.
To my wife Anne, who walked the walks with me and whose help has made a valuable contribution to this book. Together we took the many photographs and her comments and observations have guided me towards the best possible presentation of these walks. Thanks also to my publisher, Keven Shevels, who invited me to join the Trailguides Team.

Disclaimer

The information contained in these pages and the route descriptions is provided in good faith, but no warranty is made for its accuracy. The contents are, at the time of writing and to the best of our knowledge, up-to-date and correct. However, the world is a changing environment and what is correct one day may not be so the next. Care should always be taken when following these route descriptions just as it should when following maps or waymarkers of any kind..

No guarantee whatsoever is provided by the author and/or Trailguides Limited and no liability is accepted for any loss, damage or injury of any kind resulting from the use of this book, nor as a result of any defect or inaccuracy in it.

As with all outdoor activities, you and you alone are responsible for your safety and well being.